GOODNIGHT DORM ROOM

All the Advice I Wish I Got Before Going to College

SAM KAPLAN & KEITH RIEGERT
illustrated by EMILY FROMM

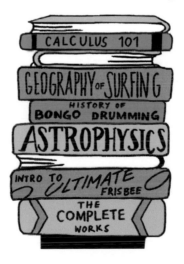

Ulysses Press

To SFSU, Oberlin College and UCSB,
We think of you always.

Ulysses Press
P.O. Box 3440
Berkeley, CA 94703
www.ulyssespress.com

ISBN 978-1-61243-568-8
Library of Congress Control Number 2015952121

Printed in the United States by Bang Printing

10 9 8 7 6 5 4

Managing Editor: Claire Chun
Copyeditor: Alice Riegert
Proofreader: Renee Rutledge

Distributed by Publishers Group West

To:

What a long ride it's been.
Such a blast, what a thrill!
You just finished high school
and have the summer to chill.

Congrats Grads!

But September is coming
and with it some changes.
Here's some knowledge for college,
the best of life's stages!

The first piece of advice
we would like to impart,
regards the months before
your freshman year even starts.

This is your last real summer
with your high school friends.
Savor
    every
        minute—
            from beginning to end.

The next time you see them
you'll have lives of your own
that are filled with grand stories
from the seeds that you've sown.

Live it up!
Have a blast under
that warm summer sun.
And party right up till
you all leave
one
by
one.

Next box you must check
before August is a wrap:
The endless business
of packing up all your crap.

So much to remember!
Pics and art for the walls;
mattress cover and binders
and pink Pepto Bismol.

For this, it's best to follow
a neat and organized list,
and check for those items
you invariably missed.

Or risk getting nicknamed
The Fungal Infection
for leaving out flip-flops
from the "Bathroom" section.

By the end of summer
you'll begin a short migration
that takes you from your couch
straight to orientation.

There you'll find skits, trust falls,
and ice-breaking games
that range from mildly awkward
to terribly lame.

Get over it! Dive in!
Let your best self glow.
These embarrassing days
are worth more than you know.

You'll start school on day one
with a soaring morale
already knowing the ropes
and some summer-made pals.

"Choose a major, your life's course!"
it's likely you've been told.
But that decision is tough
even for a thirty-year-old.

Folks steer you to engineering—
maybe health care.
"The more useful the major,
the better you'll fare!"

PREHISTORIC LOBSTER FRAGMENTS

Truth is, college is mainly
about making it through.
So choose something that meets
the interests of YOU!

Trust us, obscure science
or ancient art history
is better than four years
of complete misery.

The day has come!
College is about to begin!
Now, let's go over your plan
for moving on in.

First, no two dorm room halves
are equally crafted.
Get there frickin' early
or risk getting shafted.

ACME
NOISE-PRODUCING
HEAT
MACHINE

COLLE

Soon, your goodbyes will be waved
and your hugs will be squeezed.
Your parents are going,
and mom cries as she leaves.

Finally, alone with your roomie,
it's time to uncover
the things that'll surprise you
about one another.

You're eighteen TOO? Studying stuff??
You read that book???
Soon enough you might notice
that everywhere you look—

from your roommate, neighbor,
to that guy down the hall—
you have ten things in common
with each of them all!!

BE MY BEST FRIENDS!
NO APPLICATIONS REQUIRED!

BFFS CHUMS PALS BEST BUDS BOYS BUDS BROS

Before you know it,
you've got an odd little crew.
Who the deuce knew that "best friends"
could be made out of the blue?!

Don't fret when your first cliques
begin to dissolve.
The lasting true friendships
take time to evolve.

There are SO MANY PEOPLE
upon your arrival.
Freshmen cling together—
it's a form of survival.

You'll meander around
in great wandering flocks.
And you'll feel like a dork
on these awkwardish walks.

All the sophomores, juniors
and seniors will laugh
as the great herds of freshmen
walk shamefully past.

Don't furrow your brow,
don't worry—don't freak.
These great freshmen packs
last but a few weeks.

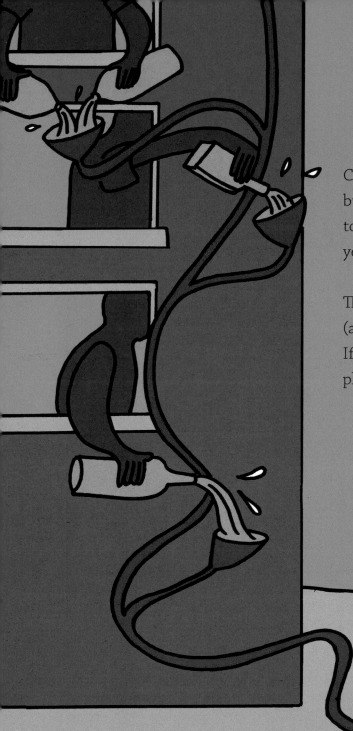

College classes are hard
but they hardly compare
to the tempting temptations
you'll find everywhere!

There are parties each night
(and some in the morning).
If you want to succeed
please heed this here warning:

Beware of elaborate
beer-bong contraptions,
stick to your studies,
stay away from distractions.

It may seem like a dream—
all these tubes and fine ales.
But headaches and hangovers
will just lead to fails.

Your roomie is nice,
he's the bestest of buddies.
He shares music and sodas
and helps with your studies.

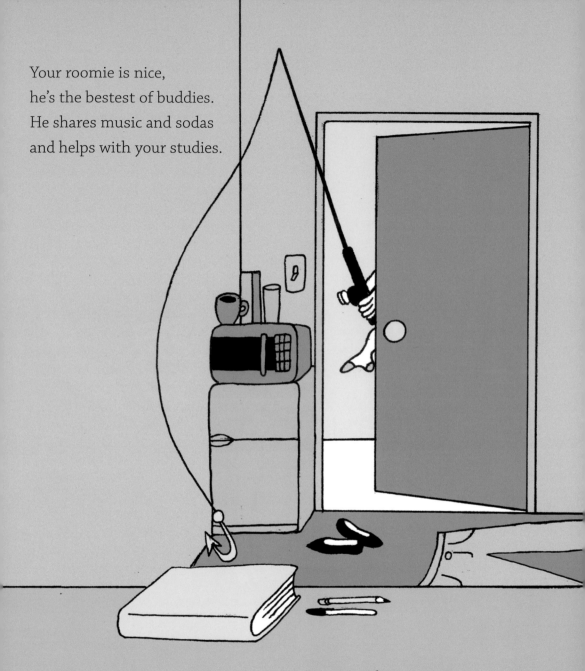

But even the nice guys
can get a bit plucky
if you interrupt them
while they're getting lucky.

Your chemistry final
might be hours away,
but your room's off limits—
there's nothing to say.

So prepare for these times
when college gets wild,
and have a plan B
for getting sexiled.

Mmmm...Soft serve! Cup o' Noodles!
Sausage pizza from last night!
Dude, don't forget to make sure
that you are eating all right.

Oh, did you catch mono,
the pox or sea captain's itch?
The dorms are simply one
big bacterial dish.

Memorize where the
student health center is at.
They've got mom's noodle soup
but in the form of Z-Paks.

Staying healthy in school
is incredibly hard,
but it's the key to
every great report card.

You may find such great joy
in your new independence.
But beware there are harrowing horrors
and stories horrendous.

Cause life can be tough
when first on your own.
You've got cooking and cleaning
and bills for your phone.

All these errands and chores
are a bore you will scoff.
But the troubles just double
if you keep putting them off.

So keep at them daily
and make a routine.
Most important of all—
keep your sheets clean!

Speaking of clean,
there's this issue of clothes.
And how often to wash them,
and how do you know?

The answer of when
is remarkably easy—
it's time for a wash if
the smells make you queasy.

But the hardest equation,
the queerest of quandaries,
is not when but how
do you do your own laundry?

What to do with these knobs
Whatsits, timers, and wires?
And how do you tell
which are washers or dryers?

You've heard all the rumors,
you hope they're not true.
It may happen to others,
but no—not to you!

You're thin as a stick
as svelte as a bean.
There's no way you'll be
caught by...**the freshman fifteen!**

But it's hard to stay fit
when your dinner is fries.
Oh, those fries? No surprise,
they go straight to your thighs.

A solution that's simple
so you don't double in size:
Keep your diet in balance
and get your day's exercise!

Do you have typhoid? Gangrene?
Or uncontrollable gas?
Didn't check any boxes?
Get your lazy face to class.

Staying motivated in school
is crazy darn hard
what with games and touch football
happening in the yard.

DO NOT DISTURB

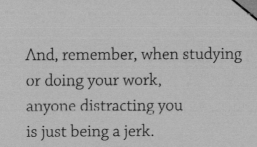

And, remember, when studying
or doing your work,
anyone distracting you
is just being a jerk.

If you carve out time
and hidden places to cram,
your grades will be superb,
and you'll never feel slammed.

The best classes of all
will fill up in a jiffy.
And those who are smart
snag them oh-so quickly.

The others? They miss out,
stuck with "Intro to Boring,"
where the one thing they learn
is to sleep without snoring.

Introduction
to
Quantum
Gravity

And the greatest of courses?
They're often quite zany.
Try one! You'll become
fourteen points more brainy.

Just do it with haste
and without hesitation.
Put reminders in your phone
so you make registration.

You may be a winner
with brains and good looks,
but that won't count for zip
if you scrimp on the books.

It's tough to keep up
if your brain is a scatter.
And you don't stay on top
of the class subject matter.

CALCULUS 101

GEOGRAPHY OF SURFING

HISTORY OF
BONGO DRUMMING

ASTROPHYSICS

INTRO TO ULTIMATE FRISBEE

THE
COMPLETE
WORKS

There's discussions each day
and a paper each week.
There's no way to display
all your thoughts if you're cheap.

The books are expensive,
we know that it's true.
But no cost is too high—
you're investing in YOU!

In college it pays
if you work with persistence
and speak with your profs
and their teaching assistants.

They nitpick all your papers
and tear up your tests,
but if you know what they want,
then you'll give them the best.

So talk to them! Talk to them!
It's worth more than you expect.
Just remember regard them
with terms of respect.

Address them: "Dear Doctor!"
or "Professor Von Dough!"
And never—oh never!
Accidently say, "Bro."

Here's a tough subject:
It's about your high school boo.
And that bad fall feeling
that you're splitting in two.

See, you chose school in Portland,
and she did the same!
But your Portland's in Oregon,
while hers is in Maine.

And despite your best efforts
and daily Facetimes,
the end has grown nearer
with the clearest of signs.

Just know in your heart
that it's no one's mistake.
It's just distance that's brought you
to this tissue-filled break.

Your heart may be broken,
tears are still being shed.
And you still can't believe
all those harsh things she said.

It sucks to be single.
It seems so unfair.
But look on the bright side
and try not to despair!

Cause college is chock-full
of cuties aplenty.
You might meet your next squeeze
while eating spaghetti.

Just beware of that coed
who lives down that hall;
that's called *dormcest*, my friend—
and it's not a good call.

WELCOME

The holidays have come,
it's your first trip back home!
Your sister has aged
and little Rover has grown.

Your parents apparently
missed you a whole bunch
cause they hugged you so hard
that you felt something crunch.

It's so good to be back,
though a little bit strange.
You have grown so used to
the lack of an age range.

Their jokes may be cheesy
but there's so much appeal
to basking in their love and
eating home-cooked meals.

It's a little astounding
how much you have changed.
It feels like your parts
have been rearranged.

But your childhood room
is exactly the same,
from the corny old posters
to your ex in her frame.

But there's one thing that's different—
that's not what you thunk.
Have you doubled in size
or has your bedroom shrunk?

Everything's so tiny
and stupid and lame;
were you ever a person
who thought this was sane?

Suddenly, you're back;
it's second semester.
You'll find that your efforts
grow lesser and lesser.

But do all that you can
to remain motivated.
Take challenging courses
so you don't grow sedated.

And one thing we know
that's most surely a fact
is that staying on campus
for four years is whack.

Plan for Paris, Beijing
Rio, Rome or Riyadh.
There's no place like home
when you've studied abroad!

Academics are super,
your reason number one!
But four years in the library
is surely no fun.

College can get lonely
when you're stuck in your studies.
So balance your classes
with clubs, sports and buddies.

There's improv! Breakdancing!
Circus and bowling!
They're all life-enhancing
and get you socially rolling.

Go do something new—
don't do everything solo.
Try Quidditch or cribbage
or unicycle polo!

There's a tough time that comes
at the end of each term
where each class has a test
testing ALL that you've learned.

You've been doing your best
to keep yourself afloat.
But now you can't read
a single note that you've wrote.

Take a deep breath.
Find your own quiet space.
And make time to cram
at a human-scale pace.

By the day of the test
your brain feels like slush.
But that hour-long final?
You've easily crushed.

All that cramming and jamming
and stuffing your brain
can be so overwhelming—
you might go insane.

Cause even the most
extroverted of persons
needs a place to de-stress
when the brain starts a hurtin'.

You ought not be distraught—
there's a trick to be taught.
Find the secretest of spots
to go when you're fraught.

Make sure that your space
is a place that is peaceful.
And above all, for sure,
make sure it lacks people.

In the blink of an eye,
it'll be four years (or five).
You'll think it a miracle
that you made it alive.

You studied, you partied,
experienced ups and then downs.
Once again, you're commencing
in a black cap and a gown.

You'll hit the dance floor
for one final fiesta.
This night's for your party
the next day, a siesta.

You'll say tearful goodbyes
to the good friends you made.
And wish more than anything
they'd just let you stay.

The next thing you know,
you'll be leaving those gates
and heading into the
great big wide world that awaits.

How you've changed! How you've grown!
The new things you now know!
There are a million new choices,
like where shall you go?

The years that you spent here
will help you go far.
You'll start a new life
and you'll soar for the stars.

Ten years from now
you'll think back with a grin
about that time you were you,
waiting for school to begin.

So let's not jump ahead
to the end of the story.
You're just at the start
of your four years of glory.

Pack up your boxes,
get your ignition ignited.
It's time to get eager,
thrilled, nervous, excited!

There's a reason it's called
the best time of your life.
It's got just one flaw—
you can't do it twice.

So cherish each moment,
remember each minute, cause
there's nothing like college,
there's nothing,
there isn't!

COLLEGE

The end...

the beginning!

ABOUT THE AUTHORS

Sam Kaplan studied psychology and balanced his studies by captaining his intramural soccer team, making didgeridoos, bowling every Thursday, and going on awesome road trips over the breaks. He is currently working toward his doctorate in clinical psychology. Sam lives in Oakland, California.

Keith Riegert read Kafka, Milton and Joyce as a Creative Studies Literature major and surfed, painted, and lounged at UCSB. He is currently working toward his MBA. Keith lives in New York.

Sam and Keith are the authors of *The MANual*, *Going Ninja* and *When Ninjas Attack*.

ABOUT THE ILLUSTRATOR

Emily Fromm earned a bachelor of arts degree from San Francisco State University in studio art, with an emphasis in painting, drawing, and ceramics. While not in the studio, she dabbled in ballet and biology and hung out at Ocean Beach. She is currently an active illustrator, visual artist, muralist, and designer in San Francisco, California.